# Skimmed Words

Poetry by Albert Haswell

Published by Hymn & Ink Press
hymnandinkpress.com

Paperback ISBN: 979-8-9929259-1-3

Editor: Sarah Whiting
Cover Art: Bernadette Beeman
Illustrations: Erin Sanchez
US First Edition April 2025

For L, J, and M—my breath.

# Contents

# Cosmic

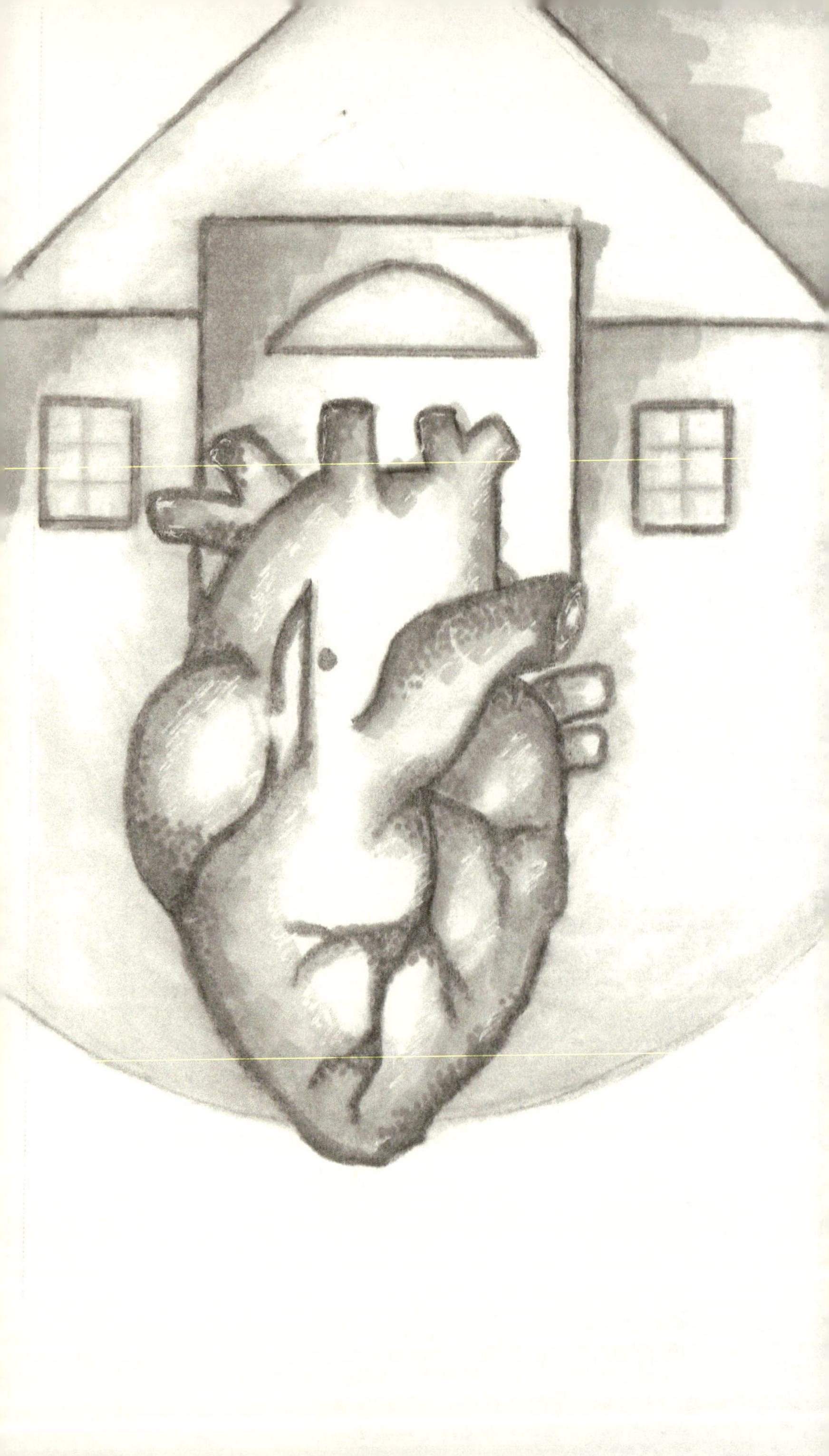

## House of Spirits

O Spirit of heaviness
the weight of your presence is unbearable.
Your ceaseless wailing builds like plaque
clinging to the walls of my heart—
it's tar-filled smoke suffocating
and staining the halls.
Burdensome echoes call out
in trampling forward march.
There is no reprieve in silence.

O Spirit of fainting, you're here, too.
Have you come to relieve me of a burden?
Sit and rest a while.
One more step and I'll become dust.
Sit and think some more.
Mistakes line up in a single-file line,
children in restless waiting.
I'm here—choose me!

Albert Haswell

A fray breaks out,
and a fire is set in the living room.
The grade is too steep across the rug to
extinguish the flame or quiet the riot.

O Spirit of heaviness—I am crushed
O Spirit of fainting—My relief is in sight

My soul is crushed
I am bound by fear
My mind is a ruin
And my heart a desolation
Am I too heavy and faint
for help?

Hands of white-light piece my chest.
The pain is burning fire;
but just for a moment.
Because the fire is that of a refiner.
The hands are gentle as they search
for the Spirits of the Liar.

Heaviness is found desecrating the halls.
His march becomes a wind-sprint.
And his baritone voice operatic with rage.
My home is being violated—
he wants me to stay!

Out, O heaviness, mourning has come!
So, the weight you sing will be lifted.
The clamor you share is now your own.
You will be crushed.
No longer inflict your cowardly sonnet
upon the heart of weary children.

    O Child—dance and sing!
    Rejoice for I have lifted your soul!
    The Spirit of Heaviness
    has been crushed.

Albert Haswell


Out, O Fainting, for strength has come!
Better-off thoughts are silenced.
The death you whisper falls back to you.
Your own slogging moans into oblivion.
You will perish.
No longer breathe your cacophony
into the ears of my death-groggy child.

        O Child—stand and weep!
        Rejoice for I have lifted your head!
        The Spirit of Fainting
        has been destroyed.


O Spirit of the Divine,
Your burden is easy and your voice is gentle.
The halls no longer fill with smoke,
but with incense.
The floors are level,
shimmed with sacrificial scars.
You have hung family photos on the walls
and have taught me their significance.

Heaviness rules no more.
Fainting has no power.

    O Spirit of the Divine—
    call me your own!
    I smile for you delight in me.
    Your Child has been rescued—
    To all my halls you have the key.

## Arrogant Garb

Cynicism robed in arrogant garb,
Claiming discernment
Posturing wisdom
Rattling off insecurity as though it were
intuition


Shimmering gemstones sunk into its skin
Gleaming abscess
Refracting sores
Sickness on display as power's source


A robe quenched by blood paints the floor
Trails of arguments
      as murder breeds pleasure
Pools of friendships
      disemboweled by ego
The reward of Pride is the dye of War

*Skimmed Words*

From under the hood leak cries of triumph

They wash across its nose

and ripple over its lips

Lies are viscous clamor covering the heavens


      Oh Creator, spare the just

      Remove the stain and stones

      Forgive us all our shining blemish

      Strip us naked to the bone

## Dragon Hymn

Darkness is worshiped far and wide
Shadows loving their ecstatic praise
Leading hymns of whispered wail
Witness! Witness! Dragon, hail!

Energized by serpent's bite
Poison... *Sorry*... Perfumed wine
Brings together the passionate throng
     See no evil...
          Speak no lie...
               Do no wrong...
The Chaos Snake is on the Throne
Dragon smoke is the breath of disciples
Look at me! Look to you! Consume worlds!
Dust is dragon food and sin his gold.

Coils couching his carnivorous creeping
Deception his voice; no ear discerning
Swallowing mountains, and drinking seas
The Dragon wins,
or so he thinks.

## Dragon Glory

Bubble, dribble, pop, and shudder
Bright eyes, crescent, a ribbon of light
    Rise above the burning level
    Ever higher, ever brighter,
        Waxing into blood moon fire


Torrents of spit and snot and rage
Waterfall from gaping maul; sheens of might
    Opened beak or snout in revel
    Inhale pride and break the bones
        Cosmic darkness roars alone


Iron, gold, and bejeweled-dirt
Clothe the beast in rare-earth mettle
    Disguised as beauty; chic—disheveled
    Wagging wealth and armor bearing
        Stars and comets hunted, snaring

Albert Haswell

Breath of mighty Dragon's promise
Burning worlds while burying hope;
Sits on soiled royal seat
Flies and maggots currency
Eclipsing moon, trick of heat


Anger, fate, and malice fuel
The Serpent's furnace flashing bright
Moths to light are near discerning
Afraid to waver, proud adorning
Death for life in shadow's morning
Death is Dragon's prize for glory

Albert Haswell

## The Valley Battle

The valley is littered with bones and empty lies
Arrows fly here, piercing sides—stealing breath
Wailing soldiers mad-foaming
from unstopped lips
Speaking once and contradicting themselves—
shouting twice and condemning their enemy

> The table is set
> Peace! Peace!
> The murmur will not overrun it

Swords pulled from scabbards
with the sheen of plenty
Only to be sheathed in flesh—
blood-polished by pomp and greed
Whispers of the slain kiss the floor—
reunited with their substance
Innocent rivers of iron gorge the lowlands—
making them sick
The earth swallows injustice
and groans "No more!"

*Skimmed Words*

Wine flows in prophetic song
The King
He has cried "*Enough!*"

Puppeteers steering violence,
Claiming devotion not theirs
Clogging the gap between dead and dying
Fear is your lover, and you have made your bed
Though your first love is pride
and she has borne you children
Blood and sweat in lusty worship
darken the valley-floor

The eyes of the One flow freely
Wind fills his lungs like fire
The throne is empty

A light has come into the darkness—
Brightly rising comes the Dawn
Striking princes blind and deaf,
burning passion away like chaff

Albert Haswell

His Voice so loud it fractures stone
and unfurls thorns—
yet wearing these himself
a burden sworn
Blood, more crimson and brighter than before,
flows from the Rising Dawn
The cleansing rain is no longer held back by
heaven, and floods erupt
from a shattered deep

Who wounded the King?
He overshadows the slain
The Voice is crushing

The water-dulled blood is offered in
iconoclastic fervor; never to return
"Reveal the sons!" cries the ground
"Release the daughters!" it pleads— "Save me!"

The Dawn does not shrink at evening,
nor the Voice resist accusation
The Blood doesn't drown the valley,
it is not force-fed into the landscape
It divides and bends and overflows the banks
giving dignity back to those who violence
raped

       Fear lies staggering
       Violence pierced on its own sword
       The slain rise while princes fall
       The Dawn delivered to his throne
       The Blood pours wine for all to drink
       The Crushing Voice shouts "*Victory!*"

Where is the hissing now?
The Voice has overcome the wailing!
The arrows cease their paths
while streaks of light cross the Valley

A trickle now continues from the throne,
no longer crimson and iron;
 it quenches the land
Clear, like his Voice;
Cleansing like his Blood;
New like the Dawn
He looks different now
He looks refreshed and torn
full of hard-earned life

> So, the table is set
> and crowns are gathered at his feet
> The prayers of cleansed creation cry
> Peace. *Peace*.

## The Ancient Cult

Cover your eyes; thin skin an acolyte's veil
Hallow the images; exalt traumatic idols
Seductive priests command attention
at altars of jagged glass and jaded harassment
*Who will bring us our icons of praise?*
*Here I am; choose me.*

They call for sacrifice; cloying incense rises
The fattened calf; I've been feeding it again
Skin and sweat are the choicest robes
Diamonds scattered in a sea of gold
*You will not deny us our indulgence!*
*It is finished.*

The meal is over; I have ascended
An offering for the world; the children
murdered
This temple is filled with a fawning parish
Hackneyed worship; charismatic fervor
*Prepare the blessing—do not delay.*
*My peace I give to you.*

## The Usurper

Usurped thrones and gold and armor
Shadows knighted into power
Swords dripping krait's hot venom
The Beast revels in high tower.

"Fear, where are you?!" cries the kING.
"Here am I, oh kING, send me!"

> I will consume them with the night
> Deliver them into thy hands
> Begging relief from dreadful thoughts
> Their daily terror is thine brand

> I will draw them to their knees
> Make them feel the demon's sway
> Visions I will dearly gift them
> Until their minds become your prey

Albert Haswell


"Pride, where are you!?" cries the kING.
"Here am I, oh kING, send me!"

    I will make them lean and sway
    and vomit in their greedy lust
    They will have all they desire
    Until again they fall to dust

    I will carve a name for thee
    Between their severed families
    I will follow Fear in stride
    Who can resist Fear and Pride?

"Death, where are you?!" cries the kING.
"Here am I, oh kING, send me!"

    No longer will the masses mourn
    They will wander on the earth
    Brothers lie and kill and rage
    Murder will be conceived today

Living dead, or in the dirt

It makes no difference in thine eyes

Death is here to set them free

Lies will claim your victory

Death will never see defeat


"Beast, usurper, where are you?!"

"........."

"Beast, I am the One you answer!"

"Here I am, oh King, mercy!"


Because you've come

against my Throne

you will see fire

forevermore

Because you've stolen

my beloved

You will be struck

with an iron-rod

Albert Haswell


And for your servant friends the same
My justice will not be mocked
You cling to life as if you named her
and spit in ravenous grasps for power

So, when, O you Beast, you
swallow the cup of your kINGDOM
All who cradle in your shadow
will crumble quicker than your tower

*Let the Beloved forever know*
*that in the wake of murder*
*The Beast is made a spectacle*
*The King has judged his usurper*

# Dust

## Holy Ground

Reddened leaves burst forth
from stems that take and give.
Catching light, eyes awake
the flame of equinox's fire.

Radiant dancing in the wind.
Resplendent image not consumed.
Reflection ebbs to incandescence.
Fading leaves to sacred pyre.

Holy Ground is shouted loud—
felt in flames of brandished light.
Consecrated dwelling sings;
condemned to death be the liar!

Albert Haswell


Temple grounds now littered
with fronds. Light sharp and piercing
the dry hide. Flames of carbon
slowly waned to compost thorny briar.


Brown and crumpled past
deceased. Alive and breathe
the dust of feet who give
their lives to autumnal mire.


Sing and Worship Bramble Choir!
Be Praised, O Blessed Thorny Fire!

## Vine and Branch

The vine winds and wraps
and follows the flow of the sap
drinking in the branch's life
warmed and fed in spite
of the nicks and shards
and occasional barbs
that lie along its creeping arms

Freely pass away the life
from branch to vine—*from branch to vine*
A graft that glues a mended break
The branch will keep the vine awake

It is the vine that needs the branch
and not the branch that flowers
The vine that fruits in evening's shadow
demonstrates the branch's power

## Stained Glass

Stained glass scabs are stiff upon the leprous
wall
Revealing a story of ancient wounds and a
sturdy skeleton
Drooping skin of lead-heavy paint in dire need
of healing balm
Scars forming through repeat offenses by the
morning sun

The cavernous maw of oaken lips grin at the
broken path with glee
Two iron teeth—with unfilled cavities
of ruddy rust
Cracked and worn by years of stale bread
and bulimic purging
Stained by the drinking of ruby wine—
Come in, kneel... pray...

Amidst the silence a seizure grips the bronze
pinnacle in predictive fashion

Albert Haswell

Convulsions pick at the scabs
and the stories are forced to dance

The scream rips into the discreet morning
And any peace is torn in half for indentured
passion
One, two, three shrieks explode in legalistic
gasping ready to inhale the faithful chants
as what was offered is now consumed

Behind the grimace of promised purpose an
empty hollow lies
A mist in the petty pulpit carries its fog into
the pews—
Pine boxes cut in half, the right way, so that
the dead can sit upright
And quiet, without a shred of their humanity
on display—like they're supposed to
Musk and mold and flies and foulness fill the
crater gut
Swamped stenches of sulfur ride the pests like
Revelation horses

The same fire and brimstone once revered in
boldness thickens the air like soot
The bloated belly, still sick on sweet-worded
homily, is ever more ravenous

The altar-shelves are full of leaves stuck
together with time
Black and green, like bruised ribs, outshine the
golden edges
Hubris has claimed the air where God-
breathed words are condemned to grime
And instead of joyous bells and songs its
loathing vile that so impresses
Threats and fear veil the ancient play—
redemption atoned for in the name of truth

So, when the scream interrupts the morning
look not for this scabby story
Run to where the oaken jaw and fly-filled hall
can never steal the glory

Albert Haswell

Pearls

Stop that rap, rap, rapping at the door!
I just want my filthy pearls.

Why won't he say what he wants more?
He must be after these gaudy pearls.
I'll throw them in this dresser drawer,
Hide them from his peeking eyes.
Make sure to hide them with a lie.

"Stop rapping, now!" I chide in stride.
As I hasten by to hide
Behind the dresser that's storing pearls.
Can't he see I want them more?

"I've died!" escapes my bone-dry lips.
Maybe this will do the trick.
Who keeps knocking on a dead man's door?
Of course, unless he wants my pearls.

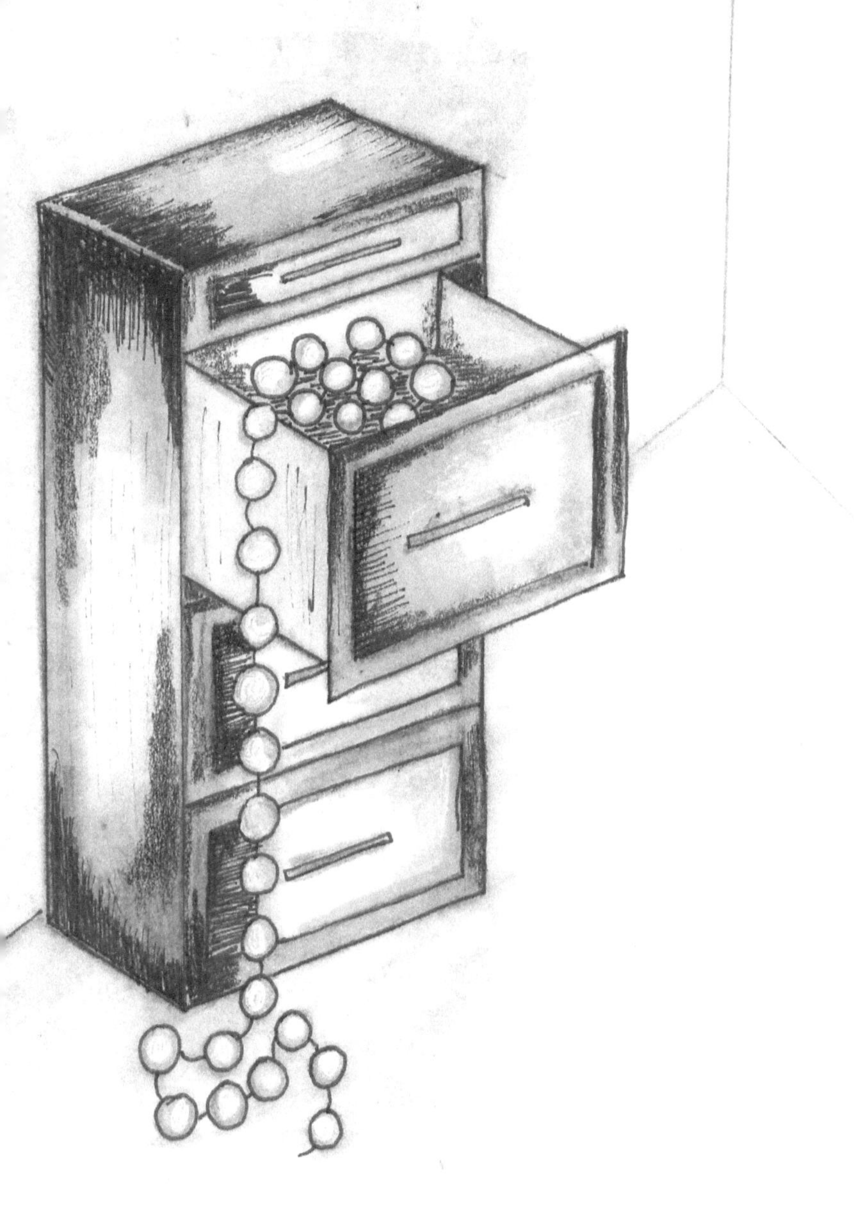

Sunlines

Sunlines race through pale blue dome
Striking so fiercely the sky bleeds white
The scattering hues of autumn heap their
plenty
Horizon lines drip with amber comb

Do the sunlines ride the wind?
Thermal breathing a conniving witch
Bright light carried through lapis bends
Seductive breezes relaxed and tanned
Sunshine wind's will-o-wisp

The fierce lines find shelter in heartless pall
Heavy clouds full of light
Stretch tightly over spinney hills
Thirsty treetops snag the cambric vapor
The gluttonous wisp is pithless in fall

Will the bright beams shelter safely?
Embraced beneath pine-filled hollows
Hunkered among evergreen frill
As quiet light's voice is gulped through air
Beams refract through root ball wallows

The tempest's frivolity steals its patience
The air stiffens and wind-swept branches
wait—
Wait in ready for the revelation of the sun
Free from the gale—a morning renascence

Shining light washes through the broken fog
Pouring out of the faded sheet in plenty
Stolen beams flow in volcanic vibrance to
dewed floor
Fields and rivers explode in daybreak choir
Sunlines, never wavering, full of windless
empty

Albert Haswell

Sky Dust

Pure white dust settles against
the inverted shell
Hammered hues of indigo-blue
Restraining the deluge
Gravity bends her seductive pull
That glory might reign supreme
More than heavy rain-bearers and shadow-
makers

The guardians of his robes
and the covering of his feet
The reflection of his radiance
as they refract the signs
of the golden lanterns
hung with precision

They follow their lines
because he's said so.
Gravity calls for them
and they go.

The sky-dust and holy-feet cover
orbit his weighty throne.

Incense altars smoke to the heights
Fears of death—of life—and crushing fangs
Promises made because of an unknown wager
No more heaviness—no more idols
Sun and Moon bow in the misty haze
Iron-weight obedience day after day

Booming feet dance through morning
Receive broken vows
And pour the rain of faithfulness
No more floods but those of fire

Dust or cloud, inverted misty ground
Obscure the heavens and sing
Of the light to light
And darkness cleansed Divinity

## Oak and Pine

Color curls inward as the wind whips,
whistling in the whims of oak and pine.
Crunch and crinkle in the sky

Return, retreat in victory, shout!
Vibrant monotones capture the sun
Shout for triumph, the summer's won.

Ready the castle for winter's edge
Hues of yellow advance in stride
Red and orange siege and chide

Satisfy the sacrifice of needy kings
dropping what was built in spring
Falling faithful oaken-line
But winter won't defeat the pine.

## Tidal Sky

Clouds are all that fill the sky
Gray and rolling like the tide
Crowded gray and white collide

Senses dulled, no corners shine
The sun meanders in awkward hiding
while crowded gray and white collide

Maybe rain will shuffle by
Purpose pouring—meaning high
Nothing yet as I survey
The colliding white and crowded gray.

## Naked Winter

A season of bare branches.
You can see how the trees actually look,
and they are often more tangled and gnarled
then their beauty lets on when they are
clothed.

But the sun shines anyway.

Clothed or naked,
burdened with beauty or tangled and bare,
the light makes itself known.
Warmth, though maybe not heat, comforts.
And the trees, though not obviously
productive,
know the sun—
They know the light, they know the warmth.
They are not sleeping or dead,
they are anticipating.
Burdened beauty and tangled nakedness are
hopefully, and necessarily, inseparable.

## Tundra King

Frozen fate favors doubt
With delicate thistle as a crown
Glass eyeballs stare with hope
As easily as the dead at dirt

Folly folds my fabled dreams
Carrying the royal stick
Gemmy pimples hard as stone
And Winter's gray the purulent

Fortune frees a phlegmy drain
The royal cloak gains its gold
From feverish sweats and shivering bones
And a poor beggar's skin exposed

An icy prophecy is breathed
So, rise, O King of barrenness
Let not the plague in your lungs
Carry you raving into madness

## Deep Well

I close my eyes and stare into the well
There is depth to the darkness, depth to
despair
I could traverse down the well's black path
and explore the splintered sides
I could rub my hands along the frame
while counting the arches and countless names
which give shape to the rickety hole
and inflicts on me this day-drawn wrath.

Scraping knuckles along brick and mortar
finding patches to cover dynamite devastations
How long can these patches brace
as the ground pushes back in spite
To go deeper down the gloomy hall
means I'll find more wounds within the crawl
with no more pitch to patch the brick
I fear the dark well's shame-scarred face

Deeper still, the dark extends
with wounds seeping muddy memories
The black-hole stones storing what was said
and breathed
I can hear the drip of leaky lies filling the pool
below
How dirty must the water be
Filled with the hidden parts of me
Years of crumbling walls dripping guilt
contaminating what was never grieved

With nothing but the darkness leading
My skin and bones and heart descend
into the waters of the stony urn
With the most faith I have ever felt
More than each death dealing act
And with more real death than sin extracts
My body submerges into the abyss
Into my deepest fears I turn

Smoldering flickers in the submerged mire
And the water begins to burn and shine
The first light I have seen all night
sparks from within the sunken heart's river
Every chipped rock or muddy flow that's fallen
That's rained with promises of death are stolen
The flowing flames of a deep soul spring
consume the mire with inspired fire

# Fog

## Shadow's Stay

A shadow lengthens day by day
While darkness settles in to stay
Visiting, an unwelcome guest
      — "Do you need advice?"
Expecting to be richly blessed

Just a few days on the couch
My insecurity its vouch
Unwelcomed, yes, but useful now
      — "Do you need advice?"
I will let the cool shade plough

The room upstairs becomes its loft
Bed and breakfast; gather thoughts
It's still unwelcomed, probably
      — "Do you need advice?"
Ah, yes, now I see... now I see...

Albert Haswell

I share my mattress with the trace
Married, full of love's embrace
Welcome in and bravely say
        — "Do you need advice?"
Never again am I led astray

## Self-Assessment

Hair disheveled and spit dried to lips
Wipe it away, wipe it away
Walk to my coping and wander back again
Mirrors don't lie; I thought I fixed that.

This time I'll get it; wash my face
Rub my eyes and drop them clear
Jog to my calendar and back again
Mirrors don't lie; didn't I patch that cut?

Bags fill with sleepless nights
And cheeks with consumed family history
But if I trim my beard and paint my face
Mirrors don't lie; who am I?

Please don't make me look again.
Mirrors don't lie; but I can.

Albert Haswell

## Gray and White

When was the last time
the path was free
Gray sky has taken its claim of the road
and the path has shown its submission
by adopting the raiment of the sky
wearing it like a child wears a cruel sibling's
  mis-sized jacket
  The whites and grays
   seem to meld together
 in little contrast
like paint bleeding on an unkempt canvas
  Well, maybe not bleeding
   Bleeding implies something
    alive and visceral
    and the path is more of a corpse by
  now.
     Did the path even try to prevent
      being overrun by the bullying
      horizon
       Did it even try to resist the
       sky

*Skimmed Words*


No, it isn't guarded at all
It's conquered with ease
by the weighty reality
of being the path
and not the sky
Hopeful meandering
swallowed up by its own innate posture
Sky has consumed this path,
and the road has given up.
The prowess of the sky is no match
for anything under its reign
It is altogether disorienting to be met
each morning by the same singular hue
as sky and path conflate their
appearance like watching an
intimate dance
Only one partner is
reluctant and awkward and
wants to go home
The stone path
wait not the path—

Albert Haswell

The stony sky is determined to lure me
into its melancholy
Its heavy and refined expression
    displayed in slate.
        The path would
            not have done that
                it winds to give direction.
        Not anymore, I suppose
No edge or turn in sight
Winter's sky seeks to blanket direction and
the path succumbs.
And so will I to the oppressive sky.

## I Tried to Catch a Dragon

It spun and weaved through medieval streets
covered in a suspension of sleet and clay.
While tracing its shadow along a narrow alley
I slipped and dropped my phone
I became a hog in a wallow
rooting for a corncob.
*How am I supposed to track this dragon*
*without a pin on my maps?*

The glint of dragon scales caressed oil-lamps
as it made its escape.
Executing a firework display in its own honor,
in dedication to its own ability to summon
affections of both fear and want.
I grab the pseudo-star and place myself as the
eclipsing moon between shining luminaries,
preparing myself for the world.
*My followers will want to see this.*
*They won't believe it.*

The monster twists its way upward, carrying
with it the wind and an evergreen army
conjured from the nearby forest.
A blast erupts from its maw; a sound like
10,000 knights, iron-clad and marching in step.
The thunder is consummated by sacrificing the
piney host in a bright orange and yellow
sunrise.
Dawn is being hurled at the shallow horizon
where I stand.
*I better check and see if it's daylight savings.*
*I'd hate to not wake up.*

## Too Tired

How many hours before the sun comes up
Various hues of black enchant the walls
Eyelids plastered shut by anxiousness
Mind melting activity,
Buzzing through the neural lines

What more can be done to drone away
Pills and purging are temporary; involuntary
Distracting blues to shade the blacks
Only seem to awaken the hive of empty,
Fretful fancy

High strung with lazy attention
Laziness or apathy drawing blood
Slivers grow roots,
Maybe artful in their spreading
Take a walk or walk myself around another
bush
Ticking, biting—he challenge steep
I just want to get to sleep

# Haunted Hunt

The haunted hunt begins again
The ghastly demon beside my bed
Behind my eyelids flashing bright
The black-hole shapes more real than sight

Movement creeps: I dare not speak
For fear the morphing scene would wreak
Havoc in words or death or smiles
This pacing ghost I do revile

To open my eyes or shout a prayer
Maybe whispers of despair
With eyes opened wide to reveal the sprite
Admitting my fear to the empty night

## Why do I have to Sleep?

I

Why do I have to sleep every night? What an unfortunate design flaw. Sleep is when my ruminations manifest into alter egos and schizophrenic fanaticism. The flashes of light congeal as though I was God, and the constellations of the cosmos needed to receive their meaning.

II

Deep fears receive faces and names. Put them in a directory or a science book. Oh, look, that cluster is Guilt and if you squint your eyes, it looks like it's holding an iron chain—or a head dripping brains.
My sextant is locked, there is no point in rerouting a course. Navigational systems are down.

III

Creator and creature wrapped into a swaddled
demi-god. I rule this world with my
perceptions and mood, and the longer I lie here
the more it becomes true. Galaxies to be
snapped away by my idiosyncratic humanity.

IV

The epic is being written.
Homer inscribed on my soul and expressed in
windy thoughts caught in the shredded sails of
a long day.
Nostalgia, Potential, and Indifference are the
Muses that direct my sunken eyes and pull at
the golden fate-strings holding these lids
together.
A world is built and then I sleep
and wake up to ruins at my feet.

V

If I could just stay awake a little longer, and let
the cosmic clusters come over the horizon in
full grandeur—because a star's existence
depends on my awareness and a comet's glory
requires my detailed description of its icy tail—
then my hopes could be achieved.
But until then, the fading constellations
remain a reminder of my history. Anonymous
altars to what could be.

## Hidden Spring

She stays hidden in seasons and in climates that
do not cultivate her promise and gift.
But, when she feels the invitation of warmth
and the season beckons her revelation she
emerges.

She will reveal herself:
      her gift
            her presence
                  her beauty
                     her strength.

Her Grace will be present in surprising ways
only to be truly seen when she blooms,
exposing the deep color of her petals
to those among whom she emerges.

Albert Haswell

Don't let the dark shades fool you into
thinking she is hardened and aloof,
Neither let it obstruct your vision by beauty to
her truer potential and purpose.
When she opens, she calls and beckons.
She invites.

She is poured out in season and when a sudden
frost comes, she wilts but withstands.
Her deep heart is given and spent on those who
will take time to notice and come close.

She embodies all those things you desire in a
flower.
She embodies all the things embedded in her
by her Creator, and she wisely bends slowly
before his Wind

## Oppressive Meaning

Life is packed to the seams with meaning
There is no room for simple beauty.
Fill the cask of my mind with purpose
and then there is no room for fermentation
The water is clear and fresh, but joy is absent.

Mission, vision, values drive us—
relentless taskmasters reaping productivity;
the new brick.
Direction—the driving determinant of success
Follow the map, don't get lost.
The adventure is scripted.
Learn to interpret everything as a word for
or against your destiny.
Exhaustion is the reward,
but we call it fulfillment, progress.

To find meaning in every jot of the story
builds and builds until the pages are full of self-
fulfillment.
Even if there is purpose on the page,
I can't enjoy it.
I am too weary from the mastering of
technique, criticism, and overbearing edits.
Beauty is blotched behind manifesting,
purpose masquerading as reality.
I become the arbiter of truth, the imparter of
meaning.
I consume the world in the name of
significance.

Beauty is not in the eye of the beholder, beauty
is innate.
Meaning often isn't because I'm hungry;
significance often ends up being empty
calories.

*Skimmed Words*

Slowly percolate meaning,
apply your best barista skills.
And critique that cup of coffee
—call it vision-casting if you'd like—
until it tastes like the dirt it came from.
Something cannot be good
unless it is meaningful
Something cannot be right
unless it imparts purpose
and drives me towards my destiny—
inspire me further and upward.

Oh, look at that sunset!
Resist the urge to make it something it isn't.
What does it mean? Wrong question.

Albert Haswell

Beauty will interrupt because it's there already;
awe and fire.
Inherent in the beams and rays
and warmth and movement.
What does it mean? Who cares.
Something can exist without my pride,
my destiny, being inserted into it.

Beauty bursts the seams and spills its guts,
let its contents flow and gush,
and refuse to gather them up.
Smile and weep in the utter mess.

# Heat and Light

The flicker of incandescence
Mechanical and precise
Light contained without freedom
To do what it desires
To warm winsomely and ignite in whimsy

Comfort rather than passion
Vibrancy exchanged for caution
Manufactured fire

Heat is contained to glass globes
Unfit for anything more than glazed gawking
Unready for anything unless commanded
Efficiency fuels the fire; guarantee the goal.

Pragmatism. Restriction.
Functionality. Control.

Albert Haswell

Now people are curious.
They are full of heat and light.

Pursue comfort over curiosity
And safety over vibrancy
Be contained in a globe of expectation
Where your flames are better kept stifled

An open flame can become a wildfire
So, contain the fire and warm your home
A spark can burn a town to the ground
So, bottle the spark to light its streets
And line the paths paving its wanderless way

If people are not mechanical and precise
They cannot be trusted with their heat and
light.

## Future Me

How are they doing?
Remember when we saw their faces
for the first time?
Those crows' feet are hard earned
Kicked in by long nights—
tears filling the well-worn channels
Do they love fiercely?
I taught them grief is the price for love
Do they look like me?
Eyes as dark and sweet as chocolate pudding
I'll bet you're proud—
I can't be sure of that, of course,
but what's the cost of remembering?
Keep my promises, don't make me a liar,
and I'll make sure they love you, too.

Albert Haswell

## The Mountain Battle

Red cheeks clobbered by windy fists
chapped skin aching and bruised.
Beaten in by Mother Nature's bastard son.
Icicle cataracts accumulate
through weepy blinks and wincing blows.
Eyes bloodshot and glazed from frozen
punches.

Purple knuckles and black fingers,
war wounds from hand-to-hand combat
against an angry February morning.
They are numb and stiff
as they cling to warm expectation.

Boots sinking into white quicksand
as I march in military stride
through subzero dunes.
The battle is nearing its end,
and I'm the last man standing.

## Skimmed Words

Hallucinogenic laughter, deep and hearty
as the deep and hugging snow,
fills my ears like the cracking of tree limbs
as they give way under their icy armor.
Memory and hope are persistent
as the caroling drumbeat crunching underfoot.

From the pinnacle point of the powdery peak
I wave to the shadows below—
*"Is that you, my love? Don't grieve for me.*
*This is my burden and my sacrifice."*
The warm air clouds of my chest
are converging around my hazy head.
Pooling into their own low-pressure systems
ready to bury me even deeper.
If I don't go now, they'll never find my body.

In my final seconds, and with a little prayer,
I lift my entire world and while my senses fail
I thrust the green plastic disk
past any opportunity for regret.

And Winter's curse is broken
as the dawn rises from his smile.
His eyes burning away the bullying cold
as if it had finally been stood up to.
Tingling limbs and melting frostbite signal life;
pulsing "*worth it*" like sap
through my beaten-in pate.

As the heavenly chariot
comes to its jubilant halt,
and the angelic shout accomplishes
it's exorcism of the cold,
a fiery voice rises up before me,
like red coals igniting dry wood in the
hearth—
"*Do it again.*"

The battle is won but the war is far from over,
and victory is as assured as that yelping smile.

## Spoiled

Furrowed brow as beams dance in stride
Waltzing streams that light up eyes
Enlightened pupils seeing true
View convincingly thorough scowls

Glazen stares can rupture hope
Bursting wishes while dreams flash by
Bye to visions sparked in peace
Amity offered in brazen prayers

Rinse them clean in parental pride
Authoring arrogance, seeking smiles
Grins pursued above being known
Buoy the acceptance of a prince and queen

Albert Haswell

## The Little One Died Again

The little one died again,
but I tried to stop it this time.
I had the energy to think about
the oncoming traffic.
So, I closed my eyes tight
and grabbed his hand,
only to see him in the street again.

## Father and Sons

Eyes imagine and engineer
they say to look, to see, to be
Brighter and more industrial still
anticipates the creeping feel

Crater holes in desire
making war with hopeful fodder
Children wag and wave and wonder
Do it again and do it louder

Fight the battle of nothing really
throwing hooks and taking blows
Bruising ego, burning quiet
costs more or less an empty bias

Wonder eyes and brighter lives
depose inhibition, engulf lies
Nothing less than prey to time
nothing less than love defined

Let the sons see the men
Not the beast devouring them.

# Wisdom

I call from the gates, and you hear my voice—
Passion rages like fire in the street
      consuming all to feel needed, worthy
Zeal burns in the furnace,
Patient and hot radiating fury
Passion rages and cries "Look at what I can do"
      "Look at who I am"
Zeal pursues past fickle fantasies
      Confidently—
      "You are mine and I am yours"
Passion doesn't discriminate a fleeting feeling
Exchanging meaning for pleasure.
      Clear a forest and build my house
Zeal refines desire—the ore for a singularity
Refining it into purpose
      Plant an orchard and feed the needy
Passion doesn't stare, frantic in insecurity
Zeal cannot look away, fading into confidence
  Don't mistake zealousness for passion.
  Passion doesn't mind sharing a bed.

## Nighttime Grave

What do you see in the nighttime grave?
    Does it wander—
        does it wave?


What is heard on bitter trails?
    Shrieks or cries—
        or silent wails?


Spirit shivers arms and spines
    What's believed—
        what's denied?


Is it good, or am I?
    Who is reaching—
        who replies?


Muddied walks and blasted stones
    Meandering flesh—
        and curious souls.

## Ship at Sea

She sways like a slow rocking ship
planted upon the morning tide.
She doesn't need an anchor;
she knows her home.
Drifting is no consequence, nor is it aloofness.
An anchor would only settle an imaginary
commitment to insufficient security.

She seems silent, unassuming, at the beck and
call of the churning water beneath her.
But she was made to withstand the curling
waves
and the blasts of salt.
The waves are her garments of pride
and salt her diamond crown.
She is weathered and beautiful.
She is beautiful because she is weathered,
like wisdom.

A lighthouse declares the boundary line,
safety delivered in warning and fear.
She knows not to travel close to the rocks.
That much is clear.
And, so, flourishing remains in the place
that seems to her most unsure.


Rudders heed in fear, and the fear is
unrelieved.
A ship out of sea is wreckage, and so is she.

## Threads

Follow the thread to the beginning,
And then follow it back to the end
Trace the knots with your hands
They are necessary imperfections.
Knicks and cuts and frays and frills
Fill the wiry, winding gist

Turn to the left and then fall right
Step forward stumble under
Climb up and sink lower
Lower down, turn over
Stand up straight lying on your back
Remember to forget, forget... forgive?

Follow the thread to the beginning,
Then back again
From red to white
From black to purple
Until you know the knots by name.
The mire and dye of the wire.

# Dawn

Albert Haswell

## Life of the Reed

Don't touch it! Please, I'm begging!
One more breath and it snaps
A small brush and it shatters
What did he do to you?

What is with all the vitriol?
Did he harass you? Oppress you?
Desire is slave to master
Skin and stomach find life
In sex and swallowing

I'm not here to touch that!
He only said what he saw
And only did what he heard
Declaring in tears all our existential fears
Consumption for life; wolves at the gate.
I am king and you I hate
Or maybe myself in a kingdom faked.

A bruised reed he will not snap

And he will not shatter injured vines

But a bruising ego he has smashed

Death to slave-master! Death to lies!

## Jubilee

Fire is rising from the city,

ashes emerge like springtime flowers.

Shouts and shrieks attack my ears.

Infants crying through thick tears.

Fire is rising from the city.

Oh, my God, where is your power?


At the gates I feel the heat,

stone walls carved with fruiting trees.

The wails are even deeper here,

as erratic cries to heaven peal.

At the gates I feel the heat.

Oh, Lord, will not your mercy speak?


Thick black smoke wafts through the gate,

as incense rises from its bowl.

I can see the tears of oppressed ones now—

they dance with smiles across the ground.

Thick black smoke wafts through the gate,

and with it the dust of burning idol.

There is a tree in the midst of the flame.
Their crowns and rights piled over its Shoot.
It's not burned alongside the chaff,
but wrapped in thorns and blood-red sap.
There is a tree in the midst of the flame,
and through His suffering love is proved.

Humble laughter loosens chains,
as shackles and slave deeds are amassed.
Children are given a future hope
while sight is restored through idol-smoke.
Humble laughter loosens chains—
His Jubilee is here at last.

## Brittle Faith

Faith is brittle if it
can't pray for healing.
If it breaks because my
prayer isn't answered how
I think it should be—
good riddance.

Faith is shallow if it
won't pray for deliverance
because demons aren't real
or it won't work anyways—
and I shouldn't try to discern either way.

Faith is immature if it
claims the deep water
and the long roads
but councils and works against
the Spirit's gift of life and rescue.

Resilient faith—
      Deep faith—
            Maturing faith—

Risks the faith they have today
      because to those who have, more will be
      given.

Confronts the world the flesh and the devil
      because resurrection says real life comes
      after you die.

Doesn't settle down in comfort but
      runs forward towards the face of God.

Albert Haswell

Bright Sadness

Dawn is rising in my mind
Scatter darkness! —Scatter, hide!
Let bright sadness grip and strive
Evening mourns the morning eyes

Dancing doesn't flash in day
It only follows darkness' stay
It comes in rising sun's first light
Red hues pulsing in the sky

Oh, dim light, remind me of
the warm and promised dawning love
Dancing carries weary bones
Awaken shadows, flee! —Be gone!

## The Light Shines

The light shines. No matter what, it shines.
Even if you can't see Him.
Even if it's obscured or impeded.
Pay attention to the light, don't run—
*Don't scatter.*

Even within a dim lamp
He is more than the shadows.
Let its brightness reveal and uncover.
Let Him, warm your skin—your soul.
And tell you with bright beams of hope—
*Oh, Beloved, I am yours.*

Hymn and Ink Press is an independent, small-scale publishing house established in 2025. We delight in working with authors and artists who may need that extra hand and support when it comes to publishing their work. Visit **hymnandinkpress.com** for more poetry and literary fiction, or if you're interested in submitting your words for publishing.

While you're at it, keep up to date with Albert Haswell and what he's making.
Follow on Instagram—**@alberthaswellpoetry**

Reader reviews allow independent authors and their small labels to continue sharing their stories and art. If you enjoyed this collection, **please leave a review on Amazon**.